# GOING TO GUATEMALA

--

A Latino-themed dramedy for high school

by
**John Glass**

www.studentplays.org
**john@studentplays.org**

# **Copyright information. Please read!**

This play has full protection under the copyright rules of the United States. No one may produce this play without written permission of *Student Plays*. Unless otherwise told by *Student Plays*, you must pay a royalty every time this play is produced in front of a live audience.

You may not copy any part of this play without written permission.

Please give credit to the author and to *Student Plays* on all printed programs when producing this play.

Please respect the work of the playwrights at *Student Plays*! Violating copyright law is a serious offense. If you are unsure or have any questions please contact us at *john@studentplays.org,* or at 251-463-8650.

# ☞ About StudentPlays ☜

*Student Plays* consists of **John Glass, Jackie Jernigan,** and **Dominic Torres**. We are a group of playwrights and directors that have written scripts for middle school, high school, and the university. We are proud of the variety of ages that our scripts serve, and we are particularly proud of our *Latino-themed plays*. These are scripts that focus on Latino youths and the Latino experience. Any school can perform a Latino-themed play: it just requires a general introduction and exposure to the Spanish language, something that most schools and students already have.

To learn more, visit www.studentplays.org, or to contact one of the playwrights directly, simply email us at john@studentplays.org.

## Notes regarding the Spanish in this play . . .

As with our other Latino-themed plays, the Spanish in this play is minimal. It is true that the play is ideal for a *mostly* bilingual cast . . . but any school can perform this play. Most of the script is in *English.* A little time spent with a Spanish textbook or perhaps a native speaker is basically all that a cast needs.

For the Spanish passages, the reverse question marks that usually precede a question have been eliminated for ease of reading.

# <u>Going to Guatemala</u>

## ☆ **Characters** ☆

**DOMINIC**  Latino male. Junior. Little confidence or self-esteem.

**URSULA**  Latina female. Junior/Senior. Kind, nurturing.

**AVA**  Latina female. Senior. Bossy.

**ANGIE**  Latina female. Junior. Angry.

**CARLOS**  Latino male. Junior. Kind. Speaks his mind when necessary.

**NICK**  Male of any race/ethnicity. Sophomore or Junior.

**MARIA**  Latina female. Sophomore/Junior

**TRACY**  Female. Junior. Very small role.

**TONY**  Latino male. Freshman. Jokester.

**COLE**          Latino male. Freshman. Sarcastic.
                  Brief role.

**PABLO**         Latino male. Freshman. Sarcastic.
                  Brief role.

The time is the present, the setting a public school anywhere in the United States. There are four scenes in the play, and each scene is simple and sparse, requiring a basic setup of chairs or tables.

** The actors performing the Latino roles do not necessarily have to be Latino but their characters must be. **

# **Breakdown of Scenes**

**SCENE ONE:**    A bus stop and sidewalk area.
Friday afternoon.

**SCENE TWO:**    The school library. The following
Monday morning

**SCENE THREE:**  Breakfast, at the school cafeteria.
Wednesday of the same week.

**SCENE FOUR:**   Tuesday afternoon, the following
week. A school hallway.

# SCENE ONE

*At RISE: A bus stop. It is Friday afternoon, and school has just ended. URSULA and CARLOS are standing at the bus stop while DOMINIC has just joined them. COLE and PABLO are standing far stage left, and are slowly walking towards the others.*

**URSULA**: Dominic, where were you?

**DOMINIC**: I had to get those Spanish index cards you made me.

**URSULA**: Oh.

**DOMINIC**: They were stuck in my science book.

**URSULA**: Well, we just missed the bus.

**DOMINIC**: I know. I saw it go by.

**URSULA**: We'll have to catch the next one.

**COLE**: *(Calling out.)* Órale.

**PABLO**: There he is, ha ha.

**DOMINIC**: I swear, those guys drive me crazy.

**URSULA**: Pablo drives *me* crazy. Always flirting with me.

**CARLOS**: Don't worry about them. They're freshmen.

**COLE**: Somebody's going to Guatemala!

**PABLO**: Yeah!

**COLE**: Pero él no habla español. *(Beat.)* Wassup, Dominic?

**DOMINIC**: Hey. Nothing.

**COLE**: Heard that the Oso Club picked you to go to Guatemala.

**DOMINIC**: Yep.

**CARLOS**: That was three days ago, man. Old news.

**PABLO** : What happened to that kid Chase? He was supposed to go, right?

**DOMINIC**: He can't go. I think his grandfather is sick. So they picked me to replace him.

**PABLO**: Yo, good luck man.

**DOMINIC**: Thanks.

**COLE**: Yeah, buena suerte! Ha ha, you're gonna need it!

**URSULA**: Excuse me?

**COLE**: Nothing. Nada.

**PABLO**: Ha ha.

**COLE**: Come on, Pablo.

*(They begin to walk away.)*

**PABLO**: Adios, Ursula. See you in class!

**URSULA**: Gosh. He's so creepy.

**CARLOS**: Yeah, you guys keep on walking. This isn't your bus stop.

**COLE**: We will. Besides, *we* want to speak Spanish.

**PABLO**: And *nosotros* hablamos español. Oh, sorry! What that means is: *we* speak Spanish!!

*(They exit, laughing.)*

**CARLOS**: Don't let those punks bother you, man. They're morons.

**URSULA**: Yeah.

**DOMINIC**: Aggh. They're not bothering me.

**URSULA**: You sure?

**DOMINIC**: Yes. But they sure as heck remind me how unprepared I am!

**CARLOS**: Oh, come on, dude.

**DOMINIC**: But seriously. I've got so much work to do!

**URSULA**: Come on, aren't you excited?

**DOMINIC**: Yeah . . . but there's so much to do.

**URSULA**: You mean, 'hay tanto para hacer'

**DOMINIC**: Right. I actually knew that.

**CARLOS**: Sure you did. Ha.

**URSULA**: Look. You'll be fine. We still have two weeks.

**DOMINIC**: Two weeks. Wow. It's just not enough time.

**CARLOS**: I can't believe you're actually going down there. How far is your uncle's town from where the Oso Club is going?

**DOMINIC**: It's not far at all. I looked at a map online, and it's maybe thirty minutes from the village where we're staying. I really think I'll be able to go and see him. But I've got to talk to Mrs. Brown about it.

**CARLOS**: Wow. Guatemala. Better you than me. I'd never go down there.

*(Pause. DOMINIC sighs in frustration.)*

**DOMINIC**: You know, it's crazy. I've told myself over and over: learn Spanish.

**URSULA**: Aprende español.

**DOMINIC**: Right, aprende español.

**URSULA**: Relax. That's what I'm here for.

**CARLOS**: Dominic, you're not a total gringo. You speak some.

**DOMINIC**: I speak a *little.* *(He looks, and thinks he sees the bus.)* Is that it?

**URSULA**: No. That's a truck.

**DOMINIC**: Okay. But, yeah, Carlos, seriously. I speak *a little.* Not a lot.

**URSULA**: Come on, let's review.

**DOMINIC**: Do we have to right now? It's the weekend. And today when we practiced at lunch I had the biggest headache.

**CARLOS**: Today at lunch you guys gave *me* the biggest headache.

**URSULA**: Come on, every second counts.

**DOMINIC**: Okay. Sure. Let's go.

**URSULA**: You mean *vamos*.

**DOMINIC**: Sí, vamos.

**URSULA**: *(Thinking of what to ask him.)* Okay. Um, con permiso, dónde está el baño?

**CARLOS**: Yeah! Dónde está el baño??

**DOMINIC**: Um. El baño está . . . um, está para allá.

**URSULA**: Good. Cómo te llamas?

**DOMINIC**: My name is—

**URSULA**: *(Correcting him.)* Me llamo.

**DOMINIC**: Right. Agghh! I'm so conditioned to English!

**CARLOS**: Well, start conditioning yourself to español. Español, man!

**DOMINIC**: Español, right.

**URSULA**:  Quieres café o leche?

**DOMINIC**:  Um, leche?

**CARLOS**:  No, tú quieres *jugo*!

**DOMINIC**:  What?

**CARLOS**:  Juice, dummy!

**DOMINIC**:  Oh! Whatever. I knew that word!

*(CARLOS sees that his ride has arrived. Begins to exit.)*

**CARLOS**:  Oye, mi mamá está aquí!

**URSULA**:  See you later.

**CARLOS**:  *(To DOMINIC)* What I just said was, 'my mother is here.'

**DOMINIC**:  I know, Carlos! Would you get outta here??

**CARLOS**:  Later!

**URSULA**:  Bye Carlos.

**CARLOS**:  Hasta luego.

*(He exits.)*

**URSULA**: Okay, come on. Keep going. Cómo te llamas?

**DOMINIC**: Me llamo Dominic.

**URSULA**: Dónde está el baño?

**DOMINIC**: Allá.

**URSULA**: Good. Okay, hmm. What else can we go over?

**DOMINIC**: Look, here comes Angie and Ava.

**URSULA**: Where? *(She looks.)* Oh, yeah.

**DOMINIC**: They get on my nerves so much.

**URSULA**: Didn't they already walk by here?

> *(Enter AVA and ANGIE. They stroll along, carrying backpacks and jackets.)*

**DOMINIC**: I guess not.

**ANGIE**: Qué pasa?

**URSULA**: Hello.

**AVA**: What are you guys up to? Did you miss the bus?

**DOMINIC**: Yes. We're waiting for the next one.

**AVA**: Oh. So . . . how's the Spanish going? Started those lessons yet?

**DOMINIC**: Uh, who told you about that?

**AVA**: I sat behind you guys at lunch yesterday and heard you talking about it.

**DOMINIC**: Oh.

**URSULA**: Él está haciendo bien.

**AVA**: Hmm. Okay. If you say so.

> *(DOMINIC distracts himself, and does not want to talk to them.)*

**DOMINIC**: Where is our bus??

**ANGIE**: Dominic . . . ?

**DOMINIC**: Uh. Yes?

**ANGIE**: I heard about that roadblock fundraiser. When is it?

**DOMINIC**: Sunday.

**ANGIE**: Are you going?

**DOMINIC**: Of course. I have to raise my own spending money somehow.

**ANGIE**: Oh. Really?

**DOMINIC**: Yes. And this is the last fundraiser the Oso Club is having.

**ANGIE**: Cool.

**AVA**: There's something I keep wanting to ask you.

**DOMINIC**: What is it?

**AVA**: Well . . . it just seems kind of interesting that . . . that they chose *you* to go.

**DOMINIC**: Interesting?

**AVA**: Yes, interesting. I mean, I heard that your uncle lives down there. Is that right?

**DOMINIC**: Yes. *(He looks down the road.)* Where is that bus??

**AVA**: And, well . . . .

**DOMINIC**: Well *what*?

**AVA**: Well, your Spanish isn't the best.

**DOMINIC**: It's getting better.

**ANGIE**: Is it?

**DOMINIC**: Yes, it is.

**URSULA**: He'll be fine.

**ANGIE**: If you say so. But it's different down there. Guatemala is not the United States.

**DOMINIC**: *(Sarcastically.)* No kidding!!

**AVA**: Yeah, they speak Spanish in Latin America. You know?

**ANGIE**: Dominic, are you sure about this?

**DOMINIC**: About what?

**ANGIE**: About going down there?

**DOMINIC**: Yes, I'm sure!

**URSULA**: Would you guys lay off??

**AVA**: Ha. Okay. Whatever.

**ANGIE**: Ava, come on. We need to go anyway. I need to change for tennis.

**AVA**: Gotta go, you two. Have fun waiting for the autobús.

**ANGIE**: Ha ha. He probably calls it the *buso*.

**DOMINIC**: No I don't!

**AVA**: The buso! Ha ha!

*(They exit, laughing.)*

**DOMINIC**: See what I mean?

**URSULA**: Stop worrying about what other people say.

**DOMINIC**: I can't help it.

**URSULA**: You *can* help it.

**DOMINIC**: No I can't!! Aggh!

**URSULA**: Look, here comes the bus.

*(They begin to walk over, slowly exiting.)*

**DOMINIC**: Finally! The buso. I mean, the *bus*!! The *autobús*! Agghh! Listen to me!!

**URSULA**: What's wrong? Tú lo dijiste. *El autobús.*

**DOMINIC**: My Spanish is all mixed up.

**URSULA**: Your *head* is all mixed up.

**DOMINIC**: Don't remind me.

**URSULA**: *(Pointing offstage, at the bus.)* Come on, the bus driver is stopping way up there.

**DOMINIC**: This is how my whole day is going!!

**URSULA**: He probably heard you say *el buso*!

**DOMINIC**: Agghhh!

*(They exit, running. End of Scene One.)*

# SCENE TWO

*At RISE: The school library, the following Monday morning. ANGIE and NICK are at a table positioned downstage, and COLE and PABLO are seated at a table somewhere upstage. There is also a third table. The tables should be spaced apart, conveying that the people at each table cannot completely hear the other conversations and are not fully aware of the others talking. However, once the arguing becomes louder, they gradually become aware, and are able to hear each other.*

**NICK**: So what's the big deal? Are you upset that they didn't pick you to go to Guatemala?

**ANGIE**: No. I'm not in the Oso Club so I couldn't have gone anyway.

**NICK**: Oh. Okay.

**ANGIE**: It's just that . . . Dominic doesn't speak Spanish. Right?

**NICK**: Right. Not much.

**ANGIE**: He's Hispanic but he doesn't know the language. And I don't know how he's gonna make it down there. To me, it just doesn't seem fair. Somebody else should be going. You know?

**NICK**: Well. At least he's going for a good cause. I hear they're going to help build a village.

**ANGIE**: I know.

**NICK**: That's what the whole trip is about, isn't it?

**ANGIE**: Yeah, I guess. *(She is very troubled here.)* But still . . . it just seems like Dominic got so lucky. I mean, think about it: he doesn't speak Spanish. He's never been to Latin America. And now he's going down there. Going to Guatemala!

**NICK**: Yeah. I hear ya.

**ANGIE**: He's got an uncle down there, you know.

**NICK**: Does he?

**ANGIE**: Yep. I think that's the real reason that he's going. But I'll tell you one thing: I have family all over El Salvador, and if I were going to see them, I'd be ready! *I* speak Spanish. But Dominic? He's nowhere *near* ready!

**NICK**: *(Motions to the papers in front of them.)* I kind of need to get back to this. Um, which president are you doing? Kennedy?

**ANGIE**: No, Lincoln.

**NICK**: You're not finished, are you?

**ANGIE**: Almost.

> *(Enter CARLOS and MARIA, with books and backpacks. They sit down at the same table.)*

**NICK**: Better get to work!

**ANGIE**: Ah, I'm not too worried about that. It's not due until Thursday.

**CARLOS**: Yo! Time for the presidents!

**NICK**: Hey man. Yeah, no kidding. So much to do.

**CARLOS**: How far have you guys gotten?

**NICK**: I've gotten pretty far. But I've got at least three pages left.

**ANGIE**: *(To Maria.)* Which one are you doing?

**MARIA**: Jefferson.

**CARLOS**: I'm doing Woodrow Wilson.

**NICK**: Who?

**CARLOS**: Woodrow Wilson. Come on, one of our best presidents ever! At least, that's what Mr. Brinkman says.

**NICK**: Ha. Right. Hey Maria, how was that fundraiser thing? That roadblock?

**CARLOS**: I heard it was hot!

**MARIA**: Very, very hot.

**CARLOS**: But it was for a good cause, right? *(Sarcastically, humorously.)* Gotta help our peeps go down to Guatemala!

**COLE**: Heyy!! Trying to study here!

**MARIA**: Sorry.

**NICK**: Yeah, sorry.

**ANGIE**: *(To CARLOS.)* Help our peeps go down to Guatemala? Don't you mean *help Dominic go see his uncle*??

**CARLOS**: Uh, yeah, I guess. I'm sure he's not going *just* to see his uncle. He's going for the right reason. Building houses or whatever.

**ANGIE**: Okay. If you say so.

**CARLOS**: Anyway, I personally wouldn't want to go down there.

**NICK**: To Guatemala?

**CARLOS**: Yes.

**MARIA**: Why?

**CARLOS**: I don't know. Maria, you're in the Oso Club and *you're* not going.

**MARIA**: That's because I went last year. It was to Nicaragua.

**CARLOS**: Well, still. What's in Guatemala? I don't know anything about it. Do they speak Guatemalese there?

**ANGIE**: They speak *Spanish* there, Latino-boy.

**CARLOS**: I know that, I was kidding. I just don't know why anybody would want to go there. That's all.

**PABLO:** Guys!!

**COLE**: Shhhh!!

**CARLOS**: Oh, yeah. Sorry. *(Turns back to the others.)* What I mean is that I'm cool right here. You know? There's plenty of Spanish in this country.

**ANGIE**: Well, there's more Spanish down there.

**MARIA**: True.

**CARLOS**: Huh?

**ANGIE**: There's more of the real Spanish in Latin America. More of the *real deal.*

**CARLOS**: I guess.

**NICK**: It's cool that Dominic's uncle is in that same area.

**MARIA**: I know.

**NICK**: I hope he has time to go see him.

**CARLOS**: I don't know if he will or not. But I do know that Dominic's nervous. He doesn't want to be laughed at by people. You know, because of the Spanish.

**ANGIE**: Maybe it'll do him some good. It could teach him a lesson.

**NICK**: Teach him a lesson?

**MARIA**: What do you mean?

**ANGIE**: You know, a lesson. Maybe he needs to hear a lesson from a real Latino.

**CARLOS**:  A *real* Latino?

**ANGIE**:  Yeah. Someone that lives down there. Somebody that really knows what it's like to be Hispanic.

**PABLO**:  Guys!!

**COLE**:  Too loud!

**CARLOS**:  Oh, would you relax??

**COLE**:  I have a test today!

**CARLOS**:  Isn't that the first one you've studied for all year??

**COLE**:  No!!

**PABLO**:  It's not?

**COLE**:  *(To PABLO.)* Whose side are you on??

**CARLOS**:  Sorry. We'll be quieter.

**NICK**:  So, come on, Maria, finish telling me about the roadblock. I want to hear about it.

**MARIA**:  I told you, it was hot and miserable. And a lot of the people didn't stay for the whole time. Tony only stayed for a few hours.

*(Enter DOMINIC and URSULA. They walk over and stand by NICK's table)*

**CARLOS**:  But you guys raised a lot of money for the trip, right?

**MARIA**:  Yep. Dominic raised a lot for himself. There he is. Ask him.

**URSULA**:  Hey guys.

**NICK**:  What's up?

**URSULA**:  Nada.

**ANGIE**:  Working on the español?

**URSULA**:  Yep.

**ANGIE**:  Better hop to it.

**NICK**:  Hey Dominic, we were just talking. How much money did you raise at that fundraiser?

**DOMINIC**:  200 bucks.

**NICK**:  What?? Are you serious?

**DOMINIC**:  Yep. Got it right here in my backpack. It should cover all of my spending money. That roadblock saved me.

**NICK**:  Wow, man. Great.

**MARIA**:  He raised a lot more than I did. Dominic was the only one out there after two o' clock.

**NICK**:  No kidding! Really?

**DOMINIC**:  Yeah, everybody basically went inside except me.

**URSULA**:  Alright, come on, Dom.

**DOMINIC**:  Yeah, we gotta sit over here and practice.

**NICK**:  Cool.

*(They sit at the third table.)*

**CARLOS**:  Come on guys, let's focus. We need to study too.

**ANGIE**:  *You're* the one that's been doing all the talking.

**CARLOS**:  Well, now I'm done talking.

**ANGIE**:  Whatever.

**CARLOS**:  I'm done. And I'm not gonna fail my presidents project because of you chowder-heads!

**MARIA**:  Hey!

**CARLOS**: So come on, let's get to work!!

**NICK**: Yes sir!! The presidents, baby!

> *(CARLOS points to him playfully, then smiles. They all quietly begin to study. URSULA and CARLOS are ready to begin practicing.)*

**URSULA**: Okay. Vamos a practicar.

**DOMINIC**: Did you hear her?

**URSULA**: What?

**DOMINIC**: Did you hear the comment Angie made?

**URSULA**: Yes. You have to ignore that.

**DOMINIC**: Everybody's got a problem with me going on this trip, Ursula. This morning in history Kyle and Sofia were making jokes and I heard them. *He's going to help build houses in Guatemala and he can't even speak Spanish!!*

**URSULA***:* But you are *learning* to speak Spanish. And you are *improving*!

**DOMINIC**: I'm the laughingstock Latino of this school. *That's* what I am! And then there's Ava's little sarcastic comments. Someone told me that over the weekend she sent out a text to a bunch of people saying that I was an embarrassment to all Hispanics. Can you believe that??

**URSULA**: Why should that get to you?

**DOMINIC**: It just does. Ava's a senior. She's popular.

**URSULA**: Who cares?

**DOMINIC**: People listen to her.

**URSULA**: No importa, Dom.

**DOMINIC**: I know.

**URSULA**: Yo lo sé.

**DOMINIC**: Right. Yo lo sé. Yo lo sé. But it still gets to me. *(Pause.)* You know, I'm not the only Hispanic at this school that doesn't speak Spanish very well

**URSULA**: Exactly. Lots of Latinos aren't completely fluent.

**DOMINIC**: Ha. But I *am* the only one going on this trip who doesn't speak great Spanish.

**URSULA**: Did you ever think that people might be jealous?

**DOMINIC**: Jealous?

**URSULA**: Sí. Jealous. *Celos.*

**DOMINIC**: No.

**URSULA**: This is a Latino campus. But a lot of students here can't travel to Latin America.

**DOMINIC**: But some of them don't want to. People like Carlos!

**URSULA**: Yeah, true. But many of them *do* want to go. And they've never even been. Not one single time.

**DOMINIC**: I know. But nobody's stopping them from going!

**URSULA**: Well, but maybe *something* is. Some of these kids can't travel because their families' papers are a mess. There's a lot of that around here. *Los papeles.*

**DOMINIC**: Los papeles. Yeah. I know about that.

**URSULA**: En español. *Yo lo sé.*

**DOMINIC**: Yo lo sé. I know what you are saying. People might be jealous. I'm trying to be more grateful that I'm going down there. I honestly am. But I just wish people weren't so critical. And I wish I were more ready for it. I'm just as Latino as you are. But I'm not ready!
*(Beat.)*
Yo voy a Guatemala . . .

**URSULA**: Exactamente!

**DOMINIC**: Pero yo . . . yo no listo.

**URSULA**: Yo no *estoy* listo!

**DOMINIC**: Right, right. Yo no estoy listo.

**URSULA**: Come on, we gotta practice. Let's get into it.

**DOMINIC**: Okay, where were we?

**URSULA**: The past tense.

**DOMINIC**: Right. Okay.

**URSULA**: Yo hablé.

**DOMINIC**: Yo hablé.

**URSULA**: Ellos hablaron.

*(Enter AVA. She puts her backpack down and sits down at the far end of their table.)*

**DOMINIC**: Ellos hablaron.

**URSULA**: Él habló.

**DOMINIC**: Él habló.

**URSULA**: Good. *(Sees AVA.)* Hello.

**AVA**: What's up?

**URSULA**: Practicing.

**AVA**: Oh. Need any help there, slick?

**URSULA**: No, we're doing just fine, Ava.

**AVA**: He can't speak for himself?

**DOMINIC**: We're okay, thanks.

**AVA**: You mean, *estamos bien,* gracias.

**DOMINIC**: I know how to say it.

**AVA**: Sure. Okay.

**URSULA**: Okay, ready? Yo fui a la tienda.

**DOMINIC**: Yo fui a la tienda.

**URSULA**: Yo compré la camisa

**DOMINIC**: Yo compré la camisa.

**AVA**: So, Dominic?

**DOMINIC**: Yes??

**AVA**: You're going to see a family member when you're in Guatemala, right?

**DOMINIC**: Yes. My uncle. I told you I was.

**AVA**: Oh. Um . . . I don't mean to interrupt but I'm just curious. How are you going to talk to him?

**DOMINIC**: In Spanish, Ava.

**AVA**: In Spanish?

**DOMINIC**: Yes. My uncle speaks some English too, so . . .

**AVA**: Oh. But it would be better if you only spoke Spanish to him, right? I mean, you will be in *his* country.

**DOMINIC**: Why do you care?

**AVA**: Well. I care . . . because, you know, it's important to represent our school the right way. Like a true Hispanic!

**DOMINIC**: Oh, really? So is that it? Anything else you care about?

**PABLO**: Ssshhhh!!

*(At this point, CARLOS's table is increasingly aware of the ongoing argument.)*

**AVA**:  Well. If you ask me, it's not fair that *you* are going and others aren't! *That's* what I care about!

**URSULA**:  Come on, back to work.

**AVA**:  Seriously, admit it. It's not fair. You know that's it not!

**URSULA**:  Ava, they chose him to go because of his grades and his work. His character. His—ahem—his *attitude.*

**AVA**:  Qué?? Attitude?

**COLE**: Trying to study over here!!

**AVA**:  What are you saying, Ursula?

**URSULA**:  You heard me. Attitude. Some people have bad attitudes. For example, weren't you the one responsible for sending that stupid text to all those people?

**DOMINIC**:  Yeah!!

**AVA**:  What text??

**URSULA**:  The one calling Dominic an embarrassment to the Hispanic people!

**AVA**:  Qué?? I didn't send that!

**URSULA**: Are you sure??

**AVA**: Of course I'm sure! I don't have time for this garbage!

**COLE**: Guys!! That does it. *(Gets up to leave.)* I'm going to the courtyard to study!!

**ANGIE**: I don't blame you.

**URSULA**: Sorry.

> *(COLE exits. PABLO pulls headphones out of his backpack and puts them on.)*

**AVA**: I'll think I'll go with him. It's beginning to stink in here!

**URSULA**: Well, *you're* the one that wanted to talk.

**AVA**: Yeah, and at least *I* can talk in both English *and* Spanish!! Unlike *some* people! I'm outta here!

> *(She storms off, exits.)*

**ANGIE**: Ava, wait up! I'll come with you.

**AVA**: Let's go, then!

> *(ANGIE jumps up and runs to join her. They exit.)*

**CARLOS**: *(To his table.)* Hey guys, we should go too. We can't concentrate in here. Plus, Usula and Dominic need to practice Spanish.

**URSULA**: Sorry Carlos.

**CARLOS**: No, it's fine. You guys need your space. Come on, we can go to the courtyard too.

*(He gets up to exit.)*

**NICK**: The courtyard?

**MARIA**: Outside?

**CARLOS**: Yeah, it's nice out today.

**NICK**: Isn't it kind of hot out there?

**CARLOS**: Relax. You're not gonna melt.

**MARIA**: He actually might.

**NICK**: What??

**CARLOS**: Let's go. Later, guys.

**URSULA**: See ya.

*(They exit. Pause.)*

**URSULA**: Boy. We sure know how to clear a room quick.

**DOMINIC**: Hmmpph.

*(Long pause. DOMINIC continues to pout.)*

**URSULA**: What is it?

**DOMINIC**: Ava drives me crazy! *That's* what!

**URSULA**: You have to get over her.

**DOMINIC**: But you know how I feel about people like her. They have influence. Ava talks to a lot of people.

**URSULA**: Like who?

**DOMINIC**: Like that girl Michelle from the student newspaper, who I hear is writing a big article about us going to Guatemala. She and Ava are always hanging out together. No telling what Ava will tell her to put in that! Ava spreads rumors. It makes me look silly.

**URSULA**: You *are* being silly.

**DOMINIC**: I can't help it!

**URSULA**: You *can* help it!

**DOMINIC**: Maybe I'm too old to really learn Spanish. Maybe it's too late!

**URSULA**: *(Closes the notebook loudly, stands up, becomes agitated.)* Good Lord, Dominic, you are wearing me out!

**DOMINIC**: What??

**URSULA**: Tell me something good for once!!

**DOMINIC**: Huh?

**URSULA**: You have no confidence! You're so worried and paranoid about what everybody thinks! Tell me something good or positive. Please.

*(Pause.)*

**DOMINIC**: Well, I don't know. Hmmphh. *(He is still aggravated.)* Oh. Yo sé. Yesterday I raised 200 bucks for my trip. I guess that's something.

**URSULA**: Doscientos dólares.

**DOMINIC**: Si. Doscientos dólares. Heck, let me show it to you. Maybe it'll make me feel better.

**URSULA**: You left it in your backpack?

**DOMINIC**: Yeah. Why not? I didn't want to lose it so I left it in here. It's no big deal. *(He sees that it's not there.)* Wait. Wait. Ursula, it's not here.

**URSULA**: What? You don't have it??

**DOMINIC**: It was right here. I put it right in this small pouch. It was . . . oh, it's gone, Ursula! IT'S GONE!!

**URSULA**: Are you sure it was in there?

**DOMINIC**: I'm positive! I put in in this pouch last night right after the roadblock because I didn't want to lose it. It's not here!! Somebody took my money!
*(Gets up to leave, extremely upset.)*
I can't believe this!! What the hell!? Somebody stole my money!!
*(He exits in a panic.)*

**URSULA**: Dominic! Come back! Dominic!!

*(Pause as she sits, confused; she then notices PABLO, who has pulled off his headphones and is looking at her.)*

**PABLO**: Looks like it's just you and me, huh, princess?

**URSULA**: Excuse me?

**PABLO**: You know. Everybody's gone except us.

**URSULA**: Oh. Yeah. I guess.

**PABLO**:  So what do you say? *(Goofily, if not seductively.)* Wanna study a little español . . . ?

**URSULA**:  Get lost, Pablo.

**PABLO**:  Huh???

**URSULA**:  You heard me.

*(She gets up and exits. PABLO shrugs his shoulders, puts headphones back on, and resumes studying. Lights fade. End of scene.)*

# SCENE THREE

*At RISE: Early Wednesday morning, two days later, in the cafeteria. TONY, CARLOS, NICK and MARIA are having breakfast and talking.*

**TONY**: How much??

**CARLOS**: 200 bucks!

**TONY**: Holy moly! He raised that much money out there??

**MARIA**: Yep.

**NICK**: But it was stolen. All of it.

**TONY**: Dang. That's messed up. I think I raised 20 or 30 dollars, total. But I left early. Dominic actually raised 200 bucks??

**NICK**: Yeah.

> *(Enter ANGIE. She sits down quietly, with her breakfast tray.)*

**MARIA**: He sure worked for it. He was the last one out there.

**TONY**: Wow. I can't believe that.

**NICK**: I can't believe that they're serving cheese toast again for breakfast. Yuck!

**CARLOS**: I know.

**MARIA**: You guys should be thankful. Some schools don't even offer breakfast.

**CARLOS**: So Maria, isn't Mrs. Brown talking to everybody that worked that roadblock? Trying to find out if anybody saw anything?

**MARIA**: Yes.

**TONY**: She hasn't talked to me yet. This is the first time I heard about any of this!!

**MARIA**: Well, I'm sure she will. She's already talked to me.

**TONY**: Did Mrs. Brown get you to confess?

**MARIA**: What?

**NICK**: Ha ha.

**TONY**: Ha ha, just kidding.

**MARIA**: You need help.

**ANGIE**: Who's Mrs. Brown?

**CARLOS**: The director of the Oso Club.

**ANGIE**: Oh. Yeah, I know who she is.

**TONY**: Anybody could have taken that money. There were a lot of people at the school on Sunday.

**ANGIE**: Yep. There were a *whole* lot of people up here. I was at tennis practice, and there were cars up here everywhere. I actually feel bad for him.

**NICK**: Well, when did Dominic find out the money was gone? Does anybody know?

**MARIA**: Monday, I think. Right, Carlos?

**CARLOS**: Yep. Monday. He said that after the roadblock, he put the money in his backpack and then he put the backpack in the backseat of Danny's car. He didn't check his backpack again until the next day. That's when he found out it was gone.

**MARIA**: And he thinks someone took it when he went to go eat with Danny the night before. After the roadblock.

**NICK**: Why does he think that?

**MARIA**: Because when they walked over to get pizza he thought that Danny locked the car. But he didn't.

**TONY**:  Sheesh.

**ANGIE**:  Well, it kinda serves him right for being so careless.

**MARIA**:  Angie!!

**ANGIE**:  Well, seriously. That's a lot of money.

**NICK**:  That *is* a lot of money.

**ANGIE**:  He should be careful. I feel sorry for him. But it serves him right.

> *(Enter DOMINIC and URSULA, with their breakfast. They have already been talking.)*

**CARLOS**:  *(To the others.)* There he is. Let's try not to mention it.

**MARIA**:  Right.

**TONY**:  *(In an exaggerated manner)* Boy, this breakfast is tasty!

**NICK**:  Quit, Tony.

**DOMINIC**:  I'm just sick of thinking about it, to be honest.

**URSULA**:  I know you're tired of hearing this, Dominic. But try to cheer up.

**DOMINIC**:  Cheer up??

**URSULA**:  Yes. They'll find it.

**DOMINIC**:  It's gone, Ursula. *(To the others.)* Hey guys.

**NICK** :  Hey.

**MARIA**:  Hey, you two.

**DOMINIC**:  It's totally gone.

**URSULA**:  You don't know that.

**DOMINIC**:  Then where is it? *(Sarcastically.)* Dónde está??

**URSULA**:  No seas así. Don't be like that.

**CARLOS**:  Yeah, Dom, maybe you just dropped it.

**DOMINIC**:  I didn't drop it, Carlos. It was in my backpack, in Danny's backseat. Someone had to have taken it when we were eating. Ha. That'll be the last time I ever go to Pete's Pizza. But whatever. Let's not kid ourselves. It's history. So much for going to Guatemala.

**URSULA**:  *(To the others.)* So, guys, what's up with the search? Isn't Mrs. Brown talking to everybody that worked the roadblock?

**NICK**:  Apparently, yeah.

**MARIA**:  She's talking to all of us but I don't think she can do anything. There were a ton of people up here.

**DOMINIC**:  I hardly even know some of those people from the Oso Club. It could have been anybody. Aggh! I can see it now, the headlines of the next school newspaper. "Dominic the Dunce loses his money!! More on page ten."

**NICK**:  Don't say that, man!!

**ANGIE**:  Hey, if that's how he feels, let him.

**URSULA**:  That's *not* the way he feels.

**DOMINIC**:  It actually is. Maybe I just wasn't meant to go down there.

**CARLOS**:  No digas eso.

**DOMINIC**:  Stop. I'm done with that, Carlos. No más.

**URSULA**:  What do you mean, *no más*? You've been making so much progress!

**ANGIE**:  If he says *no más*, then he means *no más*.

**DOMINIC**:  Exactly. No more Spanish. I'm done.

**CARLOS**:  Dude!!

**URSULA**: I can't believe what I'm hearing !! They still might find your money.

*(Enter AVA, carrying her breakfast.)*

**MARIA**: Yeah!

**DOMINIC**: And what if they don't? That was the only spending money that I had. You know my family can't afford to give me any.

**AVA**: Dang, am I entering the debate club here? What's up?

**DOMINIC**: Oh, you know what's up! My money was stolen. Everybody on campus knows.

**AVA**: Oh yeah, that. Ha. Oh well.

**DOMINIC**: *Oh well* is right. I hope you're happy I'm not going on that trip.

**AVA**: Huh??

**DOMINIC**: You heard me. You got your wish, Mrs. Ava. This Latino won't be going to Guatemala!

**AVA**: Well, you weren't ready for it anyway.

**DOMINIC**: What?? I *was* ready for it!

**AVA**: Please . . .

**DOMINIC**: My Spanish may not be as good as yours but it's better than it was last week.

**TONY**: That's right!

**AVA**: How do *we* know that your Spanish is better??

**DOMINIC**: Who cares if *you* know it or not!! *I* know that it is. And it's only going to get better! No thanks to bullies like you! *(He stands up to leave.)*

**CARLOS**: Wow. He's finally standing up for himself.

**DOMINIC**: I'm outta here!

**AVA**: Fine with me.

**ANGIE**: Me too.

**MARIA**: Dominic, where are you going?

**DOMINIC**: Outside! Anywhere but in here!!

  *(He exits.)*

**CARLOS**: Man!

**NICK**: Hey, wait up, dude!
  *(He gets and follows Dominic)*

**CARLOS**: Let him go, Nick.

**TONY**: Yeah, Nick

**NICK**: Dominic!

*(NICK exits, trying to wave him down.)*

**CARLOS**: Nick! Let him be alone!

**AVA**: Well, so much for that. Who cares, anyway?? Like I said, I don't think he was ready for that trip.

**URSULA**: Do you ever have anything nice to say? Ever??

**AVA**: Excuse me? Ursula, it's not my fault that dummy lost his money.

**CARLOS**: He didn't lose it.

**AVA**: How do we know that?? Everybody wants to blame somebody else!! But maybe he just lost it.

**ANGIE**: Exactamente!

**TONY**: I don't think he lost it.

**CARLOS**: Yeah, the window of time is too small to lose something like that.

**AVA**: Huh?

**ANGIE**:  Yeah, what does that mean?

**CARLOS**:  He barely had that money, right? Maybe a few hours?

**TONY**:  True.

**CARLOS**:  And then it was gone, that quickly?? Weird.

**AVA**:  Well, I don't know what you guys are looking at me for.

**TONY**:  I'm not looking at you.

**AVA**:  Well, in case you are, I was at home. Watching my novelas.

**TONY**:  Are you sure?

**AVA**:  What are you, a judge? Of course I'm sure. And unless I'm mistaken *you're* in the Oso Club.

**TONY**:  Um, right.

**AVA**:  And weren't you up here this past weekend, at that ridiculous fundraiser? At that roadblock?

**TONY**:  Aw, come on, I'm just a lowly freshman. I wouldn't take that money!

**AVA**:  You might.

**ANGIE**: Yep.

**URSULA**: Guys, quit. Tony, you and I don't always get along but everybody knows that you didn't take it.

**TONY**: *(To AVA.)* See?

**AVA**: Oh whatever.

**ANGIE**: Maria, weren't you at the roadblock too?

**MARIA**: Yes. You saw me - you know that I was up here.

**TONY**: *(To MARIA.)* Well?

**MARIA**: Well *what*?

**CARLOS**: Guys, can we please stop all this! Seriously. It's too early in the morning to be accusing each other like this.

**TONY**: Well, what time can we start then? During lunch? Ha!

**URSULA**: Carlos is right. Let's just drop it.

**ANGIE**: Yeah. Drop the whole thing.

**MARIA**: I agree.

**ANGIE**: It's too early for all of that.

**TONY**: Well, hang on Miss Angie. The spotlight's on you. *(He mimes holding a fake microphone.)* Just where were *you* Sunday afternoon?

**ANGIE**: Cut it out. I'm trying to eat my breakfast.

**TONY**: Answer the question, Mrs. Gonzalez.

**ANGIE**: Will you stop?

> *(Enter TRACY, carrying a book. URSULA should be seated so TRACY is very close to her upon her entrance.)*

**CARLOS**: Yeah, chill, Tony.

**TONY**: Dónde estabas, señorita??

**ANGIE**: *(Gradually getting worked up.)* Quit.

**URSULA**: Hey Tracy.

**TRACY**: Hello.

**TONY**: Come on, where were you, missie?

**ANGIE**: Playing tennis!

**TRACY**: Here's that book. *(Hands the book to URSULA, quickly waves to the others.)*

**URSULA**: Thanks.

**TONY**:  Are you sure that's where you were??

**ANGIE**:  Yes I'm sure! I was at tennis practice. Geez!!

**TRACY:**  You guys arguing about that stolen money?

**CARLOS**:  Yeah, it's like Judge Judy in here.

**TONY**:  Is that *really* where you were??

**ANGIE**:  YES!!

**TRACY:**  *(Turning to leave.)* Well, I gotta go.

**URSULA**:  Thanks.

**ANGIE**:  I was at TENNIS PRACTICE on Sunday!

**TONY**:  Okay, okay, you've told us. Only a million times!

**ANGIE** :  How many times do I have to repeat myself??

    *(TRACY comes to a stop. Beat.)*

**TRACY:**  Wait . . . *huh*?

**ANGIE**:  What?

**TRACY:** *(To ANGIE.)* You were at tennis practice? Is that what you just said?

**ANGIE:** Yes. I keep telling this idiot.

**TRACY:** Sunday afternoon? During that roadblock?

**ANGIE:** Yeah. Why?

**TRACY:** Angie, there was no tennis practice on Sunday.

**ANGIE:** What are you talking about?

**MARIA:** Tracy, Angie's on the tennis team. I saw her up here.

**TRACY:** No, I'm telling you, there *was* no practice Sunday. They cancelled it Saturday. Gary told me.

**ANGIE:** What?

**TRACY:** Gary and I went to the movies Sunday afternoon because they cancelled practice. I was at his house on Saturday and I sat there and read the email over his shoulder: *No tennis practice on Sunday.* The coach emailed the whole tennis team.

**ANGIE:** Oh . . .

*(Long, awkward pause. Everybody turns to face ANGIE.)*

**URSULA**:  Angie, you were on campus Sunday afternoon?

**ANGIE**:  Uh. Yeah.

**MARIA**:  I saw you up here. But . . . you obviously weren't here for tennis practice. So . . .

**URSULA**:  Why were you here?

**ANGIE**:  Um . . .

**TONY**:  Busted!!

**CARLOS**:  Tony!! Stop!

**URSULA**:  Why were you up here, Angie? If they cancelled practice, why were you at the school?

**ANGIE**:  *(Getting up quickly to leave.)* I . . . I have to go.

**TONY**:  Wow.

*(ANGIE exits in a hurry.)*

**URSULA**:  Angie!!

**ANGIE:**  Gotta go.

**CARLOS**:  Angie, wait . . .

**MARIA:**  Oh, I can't believe this.

**URSULA**: Angie!!

*(They look at each other in complete shock. End of SCENE THREE.)*

# SCENE FOUR

*At RISE: Tuesday afternoon, the next week, in a school hallway at school. CARLOS, DOMINIC, and MARIA are all standing, and looking at a letter and picture that DOMINIC is holding. They are all carrying books or backpacks.*

**CARLOS**: He sent you an actual letter?? People still write those things?

**DOMINIC**: Carlos, he lives in rural Guatemala. He doesn't have the Internet or anything like that.

**MARIA**: Yeah.

**CARLOS**: Wow.

**MARIA**: That's a great picture of him, Dominic.

**CARLOS**: Is that his house? Behind him?

**DOMINIC**: Yes.

**CARLOS**: Man! It's tiny!

**DOMINIC**: He says that he's happy I'm coming down there.

**CARLOS**: Oh. *(Points to the letter.)* Dominic, you can read that?

**DOMINIC**: Yes!! Come on, give me *some* credit.

**MARIA**: He's been working hard, Carlos. He can read anything in Spanish!

**DOMINIC**: Well. Not *anything*.

**MARIA**: Almost anything.

**CARLOS**: Hmm. Unbelievable. An actual letter from Guatemala.

**MARIA**: You act like you've never seen a letter before.

**CARLOS**: Well, it's just different . . . I speak Spanish, but I've never seen *anything* first-hand like this from Latin America. A picture and a handwritten letter! And to be honest, I thought everybody used e-mail.

*(Enter TONY, carrying his backpack.)*

**MARIA**: No. Of course not.

**CARLOS**: I've been living in a cave, I guess. Here, let me see that pic again, Dom. *(Takes it and studies it.)*

**TONY**: Guys, guess who's here?

**MARIA**: Who?

**DOMINIC**: Ursula? I hope so. She's late for our tutoring.

**TONY**: No, it's Angie.

**DOMINIC**: What?

**MARIA**: Here at the school?

**TONY**: Yep. I just saw her at her locker. She's got some nerve.

**MARIA**: Tony! She goes to school here!!

**TONY**: Well, whatever.

**DOMINIC**: What do you expect her to do? She was out for the last 3 or 4 days.

**TONY**: I don't know. *(Beat. He looks at CARLOS.)* What's up with you?

**DOMINIC**: Nothing. *(He hands the picture back to DOMINIC.)* I think I just realized I wasn't as smart as I thought I was.

**TONY**: Oh. I could have told you that.

**MARIA**: Tony, come on, we have drama class.

*(MARIA and TONY begin to exit. Enter ANGIE. DOMINIC notices her enter. The others generally pretend not to see her.)*

**TONY**: Drama! Uggh! I totally lost my script for that assignment.

**CARLOS**: I've got chemistry class. Later. *(He exits, still somewhat dazed.)*

**MARIA**: You want to walk with us, Dom?

**DOMINIC**: *(Looking at ANGIE.)* No, I'm gonna wait for Ursula here. You guys go ahead.

**MARIA**: Okay. Come on, Tony. We're late.

**TONY**: See ya, Dominic. Watch your wallet, man!!

**MARIA**: Tony!!

*(MARIA and TONY exit. DOMINIC looks at ANGIE apologetically.)*

**DOMINIC**: Ahhh, sorry. You know how Tony is.

**ANGIE**: I totally deserve it.

**DOMINIC**: Huh?

**ANGIE**:  I totally deserve what he just said. I brought it upon myself.

**DOMINIC**:  Oh. Well . . .

**ANGIE**:  Dominic? I . . . cannot tell you how sorry I am. There's just no way. I lost my mind. I really did.

**DOMINIC**:  It's okay.

**ANGIE**:  And look, hear me out for a minute. This is important. I don't know if you know all of this or not but . . . it wasn't about the money. It wasn't—

**DOMINIC**:  I know that, Angie. I heard.

**ANGIE**:  Whaat??

**DOMINIC**:  Yeah. Your parents called my parents.

**ANGIE**:  Are you serious?? I didn't know that.

**DOMINIC**:  Yes. They talked for a long time.

**ANGIE**:  Oh, my life is ruined!! Everybody thinks I'm a thief!!

**DOMINIC**:  Oh, come on. It's not *that* bad.

**ANGIE**:  Ohhhh!!

**DOMINIC**: It'll be fine, Angie.

*(Beat. She calms down a bit.)*

**ANGIE**: Well. I just hope you can believe it. It honestly wasn't about the money. My family is a mess, Dominic. An absolute mess. I have cousins and uncles and aunts all over El Salvador and I haven't seen them in years.

**DOMINIC**: Really?

**ANGIE**: My older brother went last year but he had a huge problem with immigration and customs; he almost wasn't allowed to come back into the country. And then one of my cousins went a few months ago but he had the same problem.

**DOMINIC**: Wow.

**ANGIE**: Yeah. It's always something. So I just never go. My mother says my family's papers are a huge mess and we have to get them straightened out. But she's been saying that for a long time. For years.

**DOMINIC**: Hmm. Los papeles.

**ANGIE**: Sí. Los papeles.
*(Pause as she catches her breath.)*
So, I was jealous, Dominic. Jealous and angry. That's why I stole your money. I hope you can believe that.

**DOMINIC**:  I do. I honestly do.

**ANGIE**:  When I first heard that you were going down to Guatemala, I thought *whaaaatt??* I thought it was so unfair. But . . . I now realize that that's immature. I realize that kind of thinking is ridiculous.
  *(Pause.)*
I hope you can forgive me. I've got to get over myself and grow up.

**DOMINIC**:  Well. You'll be able to see your family in El Salvador again, Angie.

**ANGIE**:  I sure hope so.

**DOMINIC**:  You will.

  *(Pause.)*

**ANGIE***:*  Can you  . . . forgive me?

**DOMINIC**:  Sí.  I forgive you. Yo te disculpo.

**ANGIE**:  Wow. Your spanish *is* getting better.

**DOMINIC**:  Well, you sort of inspired me.

**ANGIE**:  What? How?

**DOMINIC**:  *(Humorously.)* You were such a jerk to me that it forced me to improve my Spanish!

**ANGIE**: Whaaat?

**DOMINIC**: En serio. Tú no eras simpática!

**ANGIE**: Awww. I know. Discúlpame.

**DOMINIC**: Está bien. Está bien.

**ANGIE**: I haven't been the nicest person. I know that. I need to start watching who I hang out with. And I've also got a lot of growing up to do.

**DOMINIC**: Well. Have faith. You know? Lots of us Latinos have family all over Latin America. We just have to maintain our faith that we can see them. You'll see your family again. Look at me. My uncle is almost 70 years old, and this is the first time I'm going to see him! You still have time.

**ANGIE**: I know. It's just difficult.

**DOMINIC**: *(Motioning for her to speak in Spanish.)* Yo sé. Es difícil

*(Enter URSULA.)*

**ANGIE**: Huh?

**DOMINIC**: Yo sé. Es difícil.

**ANGIE**: Ha. That's right. *Es difícil.*

**URSULA**: Is Dominic teaching you Spanish?

**DOMINIC**: I don't think so! Angie's Spanish is pretty good.

**ANGIE**: Well, not always. Hi Ursula.

**URSULA**: Hola.

**ANGIE**: We were just talking about . . . everything.

**URSULA**: Okay. Cool.

**ANGIE**: I need to go. I have to meet with the principal again and try to work everything out.

**DOMINIC**: Oh.

**ANGIE**: But more importantly . . .
    *(Slowly and profoundly.)*
I need to get myself worked out.
    *(Pause.)*
And it might take a little while.
    *(Pause. She begins to exit.)*
Bye guys.

**URSULA**: Hasta luego, Angie.

**DOMINIC**: Adiós.

    *(ANGIE exits.)*

**URSULA**: Wow. How did that go?

**DOMINIC**: Oh. Actually, not too bad. She's very sorry.

**URSULA**: Hmmph. I bet she is.

**DOMINIC**: No, seriously, I really think she is. She seems to really regret taking my money.

**URSULA**: You got it back, right? Your money?

**DOMINIC**: Yep. Most of it.

**URSULA**: Whaat??

**DOMINIC**: Estoy bromeando. I'm kidding! She returned the money to the principal, and he gave it to my parents.

**URSULA**: Tú estás bromeando, okay. Wow, you knew how to say that.

**DOMINIC**: *(Humorously.)* I know *everything*.

**URSULA**: Yo conozco todo.

**DOMINIC**: Yo conozco todo!!

*(Pause as they laugh.)*

**URSULA**: Well . . . ready to practice?

**DOMINIC**: Sí.

**URSULA**: But first . . . I just want to tell you: everybody is really proud of you.

**DOMINIC**: For . . . ?

**URSULA**: For how far you've come. Your Spanish is so much better. You've been practicing, and working hard, and you really have improved.

**DOMINIC**: Well. It's not anything like yours or some of the others.

**URSULA**: But you know what they say: it's never too late to start. You really have come a long way, Dominic.
    *(Beat.)*
And also . . . you stood up for yourself. You stopped letting those girls bully you around.

**DOMINIC**: Ha. Bullies. Yeah, I guess I never thought about them as bullies. Until I called Ava that!

**URSULA**: The truth sometimes hurts.

**DOMINIC**: Wow. These last few weeks have been a real eye-opener for me. They really have. What Angie did was flat-out wrong.

**URSULA**: Yep.

**DOMINIC**:  Yep. But I think I understand now . . . how there really are a lot of people like her out there. Angie misses her cousins, and her family. She didn't ask to be born in her situation. There are a lot of Latinos like her in this country. And now, more than ever, I really am extra-grateful for the chance I have to travel to Latin America. I know that a lot of Hispanics out there don't have this chance that I have.

*(Pause. He looks at her.)*

**URSULA**:  Yeah. Great. Um. Are you done?

**DOMINIC**:  *(Incredulous.)* Huhhh?

**URSULA**:  If you're done, then we need to practice!!

**DOMINIC**:  Okay. Sure.

**URSULA:**  You know, ha, your little speech there . . .

**DOMINIC**:  Cállate . . . lista para practicar?

**URSULA**:  Ha! Sí. Lista.

**DOMINIC**:  Okay, vamos.
*(They begin to slowly exit.)*
Yo necesito practicar.

**URSULA**:  Adónde vamos?

**DOMINIC**: A la biblioteca. *(Beat. He sees something in the distance.)* Oh, look. Is that Pablo?

**URSULA**: Where?

**DOMINIC**: Over there. Here he comes.

**URSULA**: Aghhh! I don't see him!

**DOMINIC**: Oh. Right. That's because . . . HE'S NOT THERE!! Got you!!

**URSULA**: Ohhhh! *(Punching/grabbing his arm.)* Dominic!!

**DOMINIC**: Sorry! Oh—discúlpame!

**URSULA**: I can't believe you. *Pablo!* Ugghh!

**DOMINIC**: Ha, ha. Sorry.

**URSULA**: Ohhh!!

**DOMINIC**: *(With great jubilation.)* Hey Ursula, guess what??

**URSULA**: Qué?

**DOMINIC**: I'm going to Guatemala!

**URSULA**: I know, I know.

**DOMINIC**:  No—Yo voy a Guatemala!!!

**URSULA:** That's right!!

**DOMINIC:**  Yo VOY A GUATEMALA!!

*(They exit, laughing. Lights fade. End of play.)*

# ☞ More from Student Plays ☜

## Othello's Just Another Fellow

Dramedy. **Grades 5-7.** 25-35 minutes. 8 actors: 4 males, 3 females, one teacher (or student portraying a teacher) 3 to 5 extras, if needed. **\*\*A Latino-themed play\*\***

A group of students are involved in a school production of *Othello*, but one of them is disturbed about the lack of diversity in the play. He takes certain steps to disrupt the play but in the end is encouraged by the others to try and make a difference in another, more constructive way. A lesson is learned, and the production is saved from disaster!

## Pagasqueeny's Pantry

Comedy. **Middle/High School.** 15-20 minutes. 6 actors: 3 females, 2 males. One student (or a teacher) plays the comical role of the elderly Mr. Pagasqueeny.

Three friends sneak into Mr. Pagasqueeny's home to get something that one of them left behind. But in walks Pagasqueeny and they must hide in the pantry! In this comical play, a lesson is learned about honesty and trust, but it takes a heated discussion in the pantry and a subsequent attempt to escape to find this out!

## Una Carta de Abuelo

Dramedy. **Middle/High School.** 35-45 minutes. 10 actors: 1 teacher, 5 females, 4 males. (With the option of 4-5 extra actors in two scenes.)   **A Latino-themed play**

Two cousins discover an old letter in their late grandfather's comic collection that they think leads to treasure! The cousins often butt heads, with one believing that he is more "Mexican," the other believing that some people make too much of a fuss about "being Mexican."  Thus, they form their *own* groups in search of what Grandpa hid long ago. But what they find is actually worth more than merely silver or gold.

# Barbecue at the Prom!

Dramedy. **Grades 5-8.** 25-35 minutes. 6 actors: 3 females, 3 males

It's a classic tale of guys versus girls! It's a prom committee, and everybody is supposed to work together but differences and opinions get in the way, causing the guys and the girls to form their own groups. One side wants pasta and lace, the other wants sports and barbecue! The two groups square off but eventually work together, demonstrating the importance of cooperation and compromise.

# Going to Guatemala

Dramedy. **High School.** 50-60 minutes. 11 actors. 6 males, 5 females.   **\*\*A Latino-themed play\*\***

A Latino student is chosen at the last minute to join a humanitarian group from his school that is headed to Guatemala. But since his Spanish is weak, he faces ridicule and criticism from certain peers. Jealousy and anger trickle throughout the campus as the trip approaches, and the social buzz of the high school becomes even more hectic when the student's trip money is stolen on campus, jeopardizing his trip.

# Stravinsky's Kitchen

Comedy. **High School/College.** 12-15 minutes. 3 actors: 3 males (or females).

Two friends secretly enter the home of an employer to obtain a forgotten object but the homeowner abruptly arrives home while they are there. As they hide in the kitchen's pantry and plot their getaway, the two talk and eventually argue, exposing the true colors of one of them. Upon their hasty exit a mistake is made, and one of them capitalizes on this mistake, resulting in his/her fortune.

# Forty Whacks

Drama. Spooky. **High School/College.** 25-35 minutes. 3 actors: 2 females, 1 male.

A pair of siblings have inherited the Lizzie Borden Bed and Breakfast in New England. Although the business was run for decades in a quiet, respectable fashion, one of the siblings is over-ambitious, wanting to unearth an alleged piece of buried evidence within the house. This brings about a chilly tension between brother and sister, and perhaps within the house itself.

## John Calhoun and a Thief

Drama. **College.** 35-40 minutes. 3 actors: 2 females, 1 male.

Kicked out of a university PhD program, a bitter and dejected female lifts from the library archives original copies of John Calhoun's personal documents. Counseled and consoled by her roommates, her conscience slowly gets to her; but as she seeks entry to other universities her luck turns to worse, and the subsequent decisions she makes regarding the historic papers cause this one-act play to become darker, if not funnier.

## Honoring the Hijacker

Drama. **College.** 12-15 minutes. 4 actors: 2 females, 2 males.

It's 1981, the ten-year anniversary of the famed hijacker D.B. Cooper. The play's four characters are attending a "D.B. Festival" and have stayed up very late, outlasting everybody else. The late night chit-chat goes from pranks and jokes to outright volatility, and suddenly this get-together becomes something that three of the four characters didn't bargain for.

# It's a Super Day at Sammy's!

Comedy. **Middle or High School.** 35-40 minutes. 9 actors: 5 females, 4 males (4 possible adults).

Jodi has found a summer job at a travel agency. But her three younger siblings can't seem to live without her! They call her at the office incessantly, which interferes with the work. The standard telephone greeting "It's a super day at Sammy's!" becomes a repeated theme of this comedy, as Jodi struggles to reach a balance between her job and her nagging siblings.

# Three Tenners

Comedy/Drama. **Elementary through High School.** Three Ten-Minute Plays.

# Three Creepy Plays

Drama. **Middle School through College.** Three short 'creepy' plays.

## Hockey Masks in Hueytown

Drama. Spooky. **High School/College.** 20-25 minutes. 4 actors: 2 males, 2 females.

Driving home for Thanksgiving break, four college students stop off in a small rural town to retrieve one of the student's old family pictures. They reluctantly enter the empty home of his deceased uncle, a former producer for  the Friday the 13th movies. Strange objects are found during their search . .  but when a hockey mask surfaces, everything really goes sideways.

## The Witch Makes Five

Drama. Spooky. **High School.** 10 minutes. 4 actors: 2 males, 2 females.

After a bizarre group camping trip, a student is checked into a youth mental facility . When she is visited by the other members of the trip, memories of the weekend trickle out . . . and horrific things begin to happen.

## Mrs. Calapooza and the Culebra

Dramedy. **Grades 5-8.** 10 minutes. 5 actors: 3 females, 2 males.

Fed up with their grouchy teacher's classroom ways, four students complain and bicker back and forth during a Spanish quiz. The situation grows worse when the friends discover that one of them has pulled the ultimate prank on the teacher.

## Raiders of the Lost Rakasa

Dramedy. **Grades 5-8.** 10 minutes. 7 actors: 4 females, 3 males.

Seven young explorers arrive at a cave in a far-off land in search of the great "Rakasa." They find what they want . . . along with a few of the cave's unexpected surprises.